HAL•LEONARD
INSTRUMENTAL PLAY-ALONG

AUDIO ACCESS INCLUDED

CELLO

JAMES BOND

PLAYBACK+
Speed • Pitch • Balance • Loop

To access audio visit:
www.halleonard.com/mylibrary

Enter Code
2660-9401-1148-4610

Audio arrangements by Peter Deneff

ISBN 978-1-4950-6087-8

Music Sales America

EXCLUSIVELY DISTRIBUTED BY
HAL•LEONARD®
7777 W. BLUEMOUND RD. P.O. BOX 13819 MILWAUKEE, WI 53213

Visit Hal Leonard Online at
www.halleonard.com

DIAMONDS ARE FOREVER

from DIAMONDS ARE FOREVER

CELLO

Words by DON BLACK
Music by JOHN BARRY

Moderately
Synth

FOR YOUR EYES ONLY

from FOR YOUR EYES ONLY

CELLO

Lyrics by MICHAEL LESSON
Music by BILL CONTI

FROM RUSSIA WITH LOVE
from FROM RUSSIA WITH LOVE

CELLO

Words and Music by
LIONEL BART

GOLDFINGER

from GOLDFINGER

Music by JOHN BARRY
Lyrics by LESLIE BRICUSSE and ANTHONY NEWLEY

JAMES BOND THEME

CELLO

By MONTY NORMAN

LIVE AND LET DIE

from LIVE AND LET DIE

CELLO

Words and Music by PAUL McCARTNEY
and LINDA McCARTNEY

NOBODY DOES IT BETTER

from THE SPY WHO LOVED ME

Music by MARVIN HAMLISCH
Lyrics by CAROLE BAYER SAGER

Cello

ON HER MAJESTY'S SECRET SERVICE - THEME

CELLO

By JOHN BARRY

SKYFALL
from the Motion Picture SKYFALL

Cello

Words and Music by ADELE ADKINS
and PAUL EPWORTH

A VIEW TO A KILL

from A VIEW TO A KILL

CELLO

Words and Music by JOHN BARRY
and DURAN DURAN

WRITING'S ON THE WALL

from the film SPECTRE

Cello

Words and Music by SAM SMITH
and JAMES NAPIER

YOU ONLY LIVE TWICE

from YOU ONLY LIVE TWICE

Music by JOHN BARRY
Lyrics by LESLIE BRICUSSE

CELLO